SELF PUBLISHING
Simplified

NO AGENT FEE
NO CONTRACT
NO MINIMUM ORDER
100% ROYALTIES
YOU OWN EVERYTHING

Steven K Craig

Contents

Introduction

Welcome to the wonderful world of publishing. Not much can compare to the feeling an author experiences when he or she holds a book they wrote in their hands for the very first time. It's an amazing feeling of accomplishment, and a legacy that will remain forever. Better yet, is when readers send an author sincere letters that compliment the contents of the book. The author is then overwhelmed with a feeling of great joy, satisfaction, and pride for the work he or she has accomplished.

Many people talk about writing a book, but it is those that are brave enough to expose their innermost secrets, thoughts, and fantasies to know what it is to reap the rewards of being a writer. We say, "Don't just talk about it – do it!"The rewards are plentiful. Everyone has a voice and we are here to get yours heard.

Speaking of rewards, many self-published authors are raking in the cash. Some independent authors are consistently earning several hundred dollars a month, while others are earning thousands a month. Writing can turn into a lucrative career or bring in extra cash every month.

The first book is the hardest to finish, but after that it becomes much easier. Writing becomes an addiction that constantly needs a fix. Millions of people write wonderful books, but few know how to get them published, and great story telling is lost.

Contrary to what you may have heard, getting published is not that difficult. In fact, it is easy once you understand how the industry operates.

If you are reading this, you are most likely a first time author seeking to get your work published. Right now, you are where millions of hopeful writers have been before you, and millions will find themselves after you.

You have just finished writing and slaving countless hours over your first novel that you have poured your heart and soul into for several years. You are overly excited, confident, and ready to embark on a journey to get your book published.

Unfortunately, that leads down a rough road full of potholes and dead ends. As with all writers, you know deep down inside that you have produced a masterpiece that readers around the world will enjoy. However, the harsh reality of literary publishing kills an individual's drive, buries dreams, and lays to rest the passion of 98% of aspiring authors, many of whom have wonderful stories to tell that the world will never have the pleasure of experiencing.

Before going any further on this path, you must first have an understanding of the book industry. It operates on trends such as the vampire romances that have been the mainstay for almost two decades, only to be replaced by the 50 Shades of Grey copycat trend. Other than that, celebrity gutter trash is at the top of the heap, and if your book does not fit into these categories, you are going to have difficult time ever becoming a published author with a well-known firm. That statement sounds unrealistic looking in from the outside, but comes directly from a top literary agent.

It is the dream of all authors to have his or her masterpiece published by a well-known publishing house, but the truth is, the odds of that dream coming to fruition are slim to none. Give me a moment and allow me to explain why.

The traditional route to becoming a published author starts with the difficult task of obtaining a literary agent. A large publishing house will not accept unsolicited manuscripts. They do not want to be bothered with the troublesome of having to sift through the thousands of manuscripts submitted monthly. Instead, the large publishing houses have handed the job of finding marketable manuscripts over to literary agents. In order to get through the door of well-known publishing houses you must have an agent behind you, and acquiring an agent is almost impossible. The agents have thousands of manuscripts go across his or her desk every month and they select manuscripts that only fit his or her personal taste in literature. Right out of the gate, your odds of being signed to a large publishing house begin to dwindle. In a calendar year, out of all manuscripts submitted, only 2% obtain a publishing contract.

Your first step in obtaining an agent begins with the "query letter" where you have to sell your book concept in three paragraphs. If you cannot seize an agent's attention in the first few sentences, known as loglines, your query letter put in the slush pile or simply tossed into the trash. Here is a nice little fact for you. Most agents never even see your manuscript. They have interns sift through the daily acquisitions, and just so you know what may really be happening as you nervously wait for a response from an agent that may never come, your future as an author might be in the hands of a 19 year old that is counting the hours until Friday to go out and party. After fifty rejects, you will end up doing more drafts of the query letter trying to perfect it than rewrites and edits of your book.

Some of the bestselling authors in history were rejected by agents and publishers. Thankfully, a handful of them went the distance and remained dedicated for many years until someone was willing to take a chance on them or great literature would have been lost forever. You have to wonder what great stories never made it into print just because it didn't appeal to those running the show.

Literary agents are on their way out and will soon become extinct just as the dinosaur. They know it and this makes it even harder from a new author to become published.

One author sent a rebuttal to an agent after receiving a rejection letter. The agent returned an honest reply saying that agents are basically only signing well known authors at this point in order to grab as much money as they possibly can before they, the agent, is out of a job.

If by chance, you get lucky and obtain a literary agent, you will then have to produce a book proposal. There should be a college course on book proposals alone for the information required in it. The book proposal could very well end up with more pages than your book. Large publishing firms want you to have an established platform, meaning you already have a large fan base built for sales. No matter which way you choose, you are the sole salesperson of your work; you become an entrepreneur, a marketing specialist, and head of public relations. It can take years to build a platform when you do not have an existing product to promote. You can build an audience using sample chapters by using social media outlets, which is necessary for any author regardless, but in the time it takes to have the correct amount of numbers that will appeal to a publisher, you have already lost many of those that once had interest in your book due to the long wait. Without a platform and a large fan base, you will not get a contract regardless of how well crafted your literary work is. We are constantly striving for new ways to build your platform, and to do it quickly, without conning you into purchasing services that will have no benefit whatsoever.

In all honesty, large publishing firms couldn't care less what the content of your book contains. They used to have pride in what they produced; however, this is not the case any longer. That went away when they stopped when mass sales took precedence over good story telling. One of the reasons book sales have declined over the past few decades is the uninteresting garbage they continually market. Publishers have lost touch with what people want to read.

Right now, you are having dreams of success with a bestselling novel. It pains me to have to burst your bubble, but you are where so many others have been before, and realistically, even if you are able to obtain a contract with a large firm, all your hopes and dreams will quickly be crushed. If you obtain a publishing contract, you might be given a $1,000 to $3,000 advance. You will have to dump your advance into advertising because the publishing firm will not invest any money in promoting your book. In addition, by signing with that large publishing firm, you will have given up the rights to your book. They now own your work. A board of directors will dictate the final content of your interior, formatting, book cover, and price. They will insist that you rewrite your story until it becomes what they feel it should be.

The company will print a small test run of approximately 10,000 copies, and if your book doesn't become an instant hit, that's it, game over. Your book gets canned, they own the rights, and there is nothing more you can do. If your book does happen to sell well, you will receive minimal royalty payments that almost make you feel as if you have been robbed. The publisher takes most of the money and your agent gets 15%. If your book is sold on Amazon, where they sell your book at a discounted rate, they also take a nice chunk of the royalty. Everyone in line has his or her hand in the pot. For all your hard work, you may end up only averaging less than a $1.30 per book. It is solely up to you to generate sales because they will not. Writing your book was the easy part, now you have to become the salesperson. You do 90% of the work and everyone else keeps most of the money. Therefore, you must ask yourself, "Then why would I even want to get published by a large well-known publishing house?" Unless you are an established well-known author, forget about making millions of dollars or even thousands for that matter by signing everything over to a publishing firm. When publishing with Empire Publishing, you receive 100% of your royalties (excluding fees and percentages by retailers such as Amazon) and retain 100% ownership of your work. Many of you reading this may have already figured out that a large publishing house is not the best way to go and you are shopping around for a micro-publisher or to self-publish. Be careful as well, as you search the Internet for options, you will run across individuals trying to sell you the so-called secrets of publishing and false promises of making you into a bestselling author. Most of them are scams designed for their own profit, not yours, and prey on those without any knowledge of the publishing industry. Then you will come across micro-publishers advertising that they take on all genres, they do not turn down any submissions, and the author will have no out of pocket expenses. Their sales pitch sounds very appealing to first time authors, but please remember, if it sounds too good to be true, it usually is. If a large publishing house requires an author to build his or her platform to generate sales, why would anyone think that a small publisher, which is most likely operated in a person's home, would be able to get a book sold?

In reality, writing a book is the easy part. As an author, you are going to be the key salesperson regardless of which company publishes your book, so don't be led astray or fooled into believing otherwise.

The literary publishing industry is rapidly changing and shifting in new directions. What was the in the past regarding publishing is no longer what will be in the near future. Digital publishing is on the rise, but for those that love books, do not fret, printed books will never go away. Self-publishing and micro-publishers were frowned upon in the past, which was rightfully so due to the poor quality of the product, but not anymore. Small publishers are printing high quality books that are equal to those by the large publishing houses. These days, independent publishers are the ones that are making the money, and large amounts of money! However, be cautious when choosing a micro-publisher because there are those that prey on first time authors and do very little for what they charge. There are even a few that offer services that are completely bogus. One in particular, offers celebrity endorsements for your book for a fee of $190.00. Look deeper into it before assuming you are paying them for endorsements when all they do is supply you with addresses for celebrities, some that may not be valid any longer as noted on the advertisement, and it is up to you to make contact with the celebrity. This is just a rip off... anyone can find address for a celebrity, and even if you pay for that information on the Internet, it is only $25.00.

Agents will mislead you by saying that large publishing houses will not offer a contract if you originally self-published. That's a lie! 50 Shades of Grey by E.L. James is the perfect example of a self-published success story due to an author's determination. The book was originally titled "Masters of the Universe" and was self-published as an e-book. It acquired massive amounts of horrible reviews, mostly noting its very poorly written qualities. As you know, it eventually became a bestselling novel boasting 70 million copies sold worldwide. Literary agents are still publically bashing the book that they all turned down. This proves that they have lost touch with what the public wants to read.

There is no reason to sit and wait wasting valuable time as you receive one discouraging rejection after another as you keep changing your proposal trying to get an agents attention. If your dream is to be published in the future by a large well-known publishing house, by all means, continue to pursue it. You are not under any contract with us nor do you have any obligation to Empire Publishing after you are published. Remember, you own 100% of your rights. Empire Publishing is a company created by authors for authors. We've been through it all and are here to save you many headaches.

The term "self-publishing" has a stigma to it from poorly produced products in the past and has been frowned upon ever since. We prefer to use the term "independent publishing" since authors doing so have created a booming marketplace. What were once frowned upon are now acceptable and making millions of dollars.

As the industry evolves, micro-publishers are becoming a force to reckon with. However, many of them only accept specific genres, which limit their manuscript acceptance and overall sales power. Some overcharge and prey on those that do not have the knowledge of publishing, printing, graphic design, and marketing. Many of them offer services that are unnecessary and a waste of money. We feel a successful business is achieved through honor and providing the best service possible. We have even seen contracts where the author is required to order 500 copies of their book. That is insane! Using our sources, you don't need to order a single copy if you choose not to.

After you have poured your heart and soul into a story that you want to share with the world, your publishing experience should be an exciting adventure, not one filled with one disappointment after another. Empire Publishing & Literary Service Bureau is here to make that journey easy and rewarding.

Do not be led down the wrong path as so many others have before. If you look around, you will see that micro-publishers are sprouting up like weeds. On one end of the scale, some micro-publishers are charging outrageous fees, and on the other end, some are charging such low rates that it almost seems too good to be true, which in most cases, it is.

An independently published author may not have the expertise or the money to do everything and has to prioritize what options on which to spend the effort and/or the money.

Empire Publishing has assembled this booklet to help you get on your way to becoming a published author, and what to do afterwards in order to sell your book. We could have put together a manual on how to do everything by yourself without a publisher, but it would consist of several volumes and you still might not be able to perform all the proper procedures. Not to mention, in all honesty, it would not be good for our business. Besides that, a book such as that would cost you over several hundreds of dollars and most people don't have the expertise or ability to cover all aspects even if it were outlined in detail. Empire Publishing would have preferred to put this booklet out free of charge, but printing costs and distributor fees don't allow for that. However, there is good news. If you decide to publish your book with Empire Publishing, we will happily reimburse you for the cost of the booklet and shipping.

This booklet is a promo for Empire Publishing, but it will guide a new author in the right direction and outline what needs to be done whether he or she publishes with Empire Publishing or not.

Here at Empire Publishing, we are a team of authors and professionals in all aspects of publishing that have been through it all. We are here to help you, and not take advantage of you as so most other publishers. Inside our website (www.empire-publishing.com), you will notice our brutal honestly and not flowery sales pitches to get you to spend money. Our mission is to dominate the independent-publishing industry and we will do so by providing the best services available at rates that are much lower than any other publisher. Empire is a publisher/service bureau that you can trust and we will be around for a very long time. Empire Publishing not only wants to help you with your first book, we want each book afterwards.

Do-It-Yourselfers

Self-published authors with a small budget or no budget at all are using the free tools for publishing available by a few Internet based publishing companies. These companies offer the option of uploading books for publication. This is fine for those with extensive backgrounds in graphic design, layout and printing, which include being proficient with software such as Microsoft Word, CorelDraw, Adobe Illustrator and Photoshop. Many authors are utilizing the free interior converter and basic cover templates that a few companies have available. This is all good too, except here is where the majority of self published authors fail to garnish any book sales by releasing a poorly produced product.

To begin with, the cover is basically the single most important part of a book. At times, even more important than the interior since the cover is what a potential buyer sees first. Studies show that a book cover has approximately three seconds to arouse interest in potential buyer. Covers must be designed with balance, contrast and be an alluring representation of the interior. Using a generic cover template gives a book the appearance of a poorly produced product and this will turn customers away.

Up next is proper interior formatting. A book that improperly formatted will upload incorrectly and cause many errors in the page layout. Some chapters will begin center page, while other pages will not have text filled from header to footer. There are a multitude of errors that can occur when not formatted correctly and this is evident in many titles published by those unfamiliar with interior formatting. In turn, many buyers on Amazon are extremely critical and immediately rush to leave negative book reviews.

First time authors are under the impression that when their book becomes available on Amazon it will automatically generate sales without any promotion. It does not! Maybe a handful of friends and relatives will purchase the book, but that's about all. Most are lucky if they make $20 in royalties the first six months and then no further sales afterwards.

If you plan to independently-publish without any assistance or support through a publisher, be prepared to put in an extensive amount of work in pre-production and post production.

Whereas most Do-It-Yourselfer's fail when self-publishing, there are exceptions, and many authors have went on to make a substantial amount of money for their efforts. Continue reading and this booklet will provide you with a guideline on how to self-publish and market your book.

Print and Digital Books

Digital publishing is no longer an option - it's a requirement if you want to reach your full sales potential. Regardless of fast moving technological advances and the popularity of eBook readers, the printed book will never cease to exist. Most avid readers have a love affair with the printed book. They feel it is a more personal experience with the feel of the pages, the smell of the ink and aesthetically pleasing rather than the coldness of a hand held device. It is simply superior to the digital book in look and feel. A printed book allows creativity with font styles, graphics and photographs were the digital book falls short. As of date, most authors are reporting an equal amount of print and digital book sales.

The love for printed books is not only that of older generations, but it is seen through a survey showing that many of the youth today would rather have a printed book in their hands to read. Even as large bookstore chains have toppled over the past decade, the printed book is still holding its ground in sales, and can be seen by the reemergence of smaller local book stores. The Association of America Publishers reported that printed books sales grew 10% in 2013 instead of falling in sales as it did in previous years.

However, indie authors are making enormous amounts of money publishing electronically for digital reading devices, and theses reading devices are rapidly growing in popularity. A buyer can download a book in a matter of minutes and read it at their leisure on these electronic devices, which now includes the smartphones. A serious author utilizes both formats to his or her benefit for full potential for maximum sales.

Digital Book Interior

Before an eBook can be published, it must first be converted to a format that can be identified by digital readers. There are currently two main formats that the industry uses: ePub, which works with almost every reading device, and .mobi, which is used by Amazon's Kindle.

There is a wide range of pricing and services available on the Internet for eBook formatting. Some publishers have automatic conversions for MS Word and PDF files. These do not work well and what an author ends up with is an unprofessional looking, poorly produced book which readers will be extremely critical towards.

What happens when using an automatic converter is the eBook ends up looking as if it was vomited onto a reading device. Words are sized incorrectly, first line indentations begin halfway across the page, chapters start mid page, photo's, text boxes and bullets are out of place, and then there are multiple blank pages. In other words, it's a total mess.

In order to properly format a manuscript for eBook publishing, it takes several hands on hours by a professional. Don't be misled by someone offering to do the conversion for $30.00. Keep in mind the old saying, "You get what you pay for."

Most other companies offering this service simply run the manuscript through an automatic conversion program.

Empire Publishing scans each sentence individually during the process and performs all the necessary changes.

Example of Automatic Conversion
(Original Manuscript in MS Word)

Last First Kiss

After a restless night of tossing and turning in bed, Anna decides to take the day off from work so she can have extra time preparing for their long overdue meeting. She arrives at the hotel an hour before Christopher to set the room up for a comfortable and romantic evening, which seems destined to be an epic, once in a lifetime event. It's an exceptionally warm summer day, but the air is cool around the resort from the large trees that act as a protective umbrella from the sun. The car keys in her hand jingle as she nervously inserts the card to unlock the door. She stands in the doorway for a moment and fantasizes about what may be to come this night.

It's a beautiful room that's specifically designed as a getaway for lovers. The living area is decorated in soft earth tones and pastel colors, complete with a large, plush sofa, faint mood lighting, flowers, exquisite wine and crystal glasses.

---

road to get home. He talks to Anna throughout the drive, and tucks her in bed via the phone. Steven and Anna both have a restless night knowing that tomorrow they will finally see each other. (1)

Last First(2) Kiss(3)

A(4) fter a restless night of tossing and turning in bed, Anna decides to take the day off from work so she can have extra time preparing for their long overdue meeting. She arrives at the hotel an hour before Steven to set the room up for a comfortable and romantic evening, which seems destined to be an epic, once in a lifetime event. It's an exceptionally warm summer day, but the air is cool around the resort from the large trees that act as a protective umbrella from the sun. The car keys in her hand jingle as she nervously inserts the card to unlock the door. She stands in the doorway for a moment and fantasizes about what may be to come this night.

(5)It's a beautiful room that's specifically designed as a getaway for lovers. The living area is decorated in soft earth tones and pastel colors, complete with a large, plush sofa, faint mood lighting, flowers, exquisite wine and crystal glasses.

#1 - Changes in paragraph alignment. Incorrect line spacing. Loss of paragraph justification.
#2 - Non-existent page break. Chapter begins mid-page.
#3 - Improper (heading) chapter title and font size.
#4 - Drop Cap moves above paragraph.
#5 - Shift in first line indentation.

There are many more formatting errors that can occur after an automatic conversion - some of which will create multiple blank pages. The most common errors are using tabs instead of first line indents, hidden double spacing and multiple hits of the space bar. In addition, you must know where to put in proper page breaks so chapters will start on a new page and create Headings. Then there is setting up a Table of Contents that all digital readers will be able to recognize. The list for properly formatting an eBook is endless and unless an author has extensive knowledge in formatting, he or she might find themselves pulling their hair out trying to get it correct.

Microsoft Word is the most recognized and accepted software by publishers/printers, but is also an inexperienced user's worst enemy. Most publishers are able to use a Word doc as long as the fonts are embedded properly. Others require the manuscript to be in a pdf file.

Please note that there are only 6 common fonts available for the Amazon Kindle. Fancy fonts, symbols and drop caps do not work at all. There cannot be any columns or text boxes unless they are turned into a graphic image (jpeg). Any photographs must be centered and in line with text with a continuous page break before and after the photograph. Photos must also be correctly sized for the digital devices.

For the Do It Yourselfers, interior photographs must be above 200 dpi, and covers must be higher than 300 dpi.

Empire Publishing uses the authors MS Word doc or PDF file to covert from printed format to ePub format. Empire Publishing does all conversions manually and double checks the formatting on a digital reader.

Print Book Interior

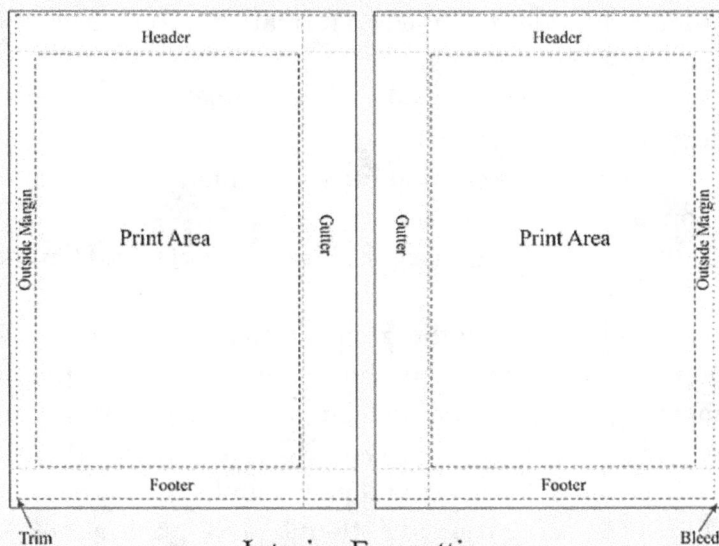

Interior Formatting

Before a book can be printed, the interior must be properly formatted. This cannot be accomplished until the font size has been chosen, trim size is decided upon, and the final word count is established. Then the real work begins to properly format the interior to meet printing guidelines.

Book interiors must be mathematically figured out before going to press. For example, depending on how many pages your book is, the measurement of the gutter will change from the first pages to those in the center of large page count books. Proper margins must be set at top, bottom, and outside for centering the printed area. Incorrect formatting will be rejected by any printer. Layout includes: a title page, page numbers, chapter/section headings and running headers where appropriate.

Common mistakes made when formatted improperly:

1. Improper Intents and Tabs
2. Repeating Paragraph
3. Hidden multiple spacing between sentences
4. Font and Style Mistakes
5. Improper Heading, Margins, Header, Footer and Gutter

These are just a few of the common mistakes authors make when preparing for publishing. The editors at Empire Publishing correctly format your manuscript and fix any errors that you may not even realize are there. We also insert a Table of Contents and page numbers if they are not included in the file you have submitted for publication.
Empire Publishing offers free downloadable templates for all trim sizes at www.empire-publishing.com.

Empire Publishing offers three levels of interior formatting.

Standard Formatting - This is included in Empire Publishing's "Budget" publishing packages. Standard formatting is performed when an author does not have a specific design or formatting idea and needs the assistance of our experts in the industry to design an interior layout that conforms to professional industry standards. We will choose the appropriate font, line spacing, and style treatments for your book based upon the package you choose and the genre of the manuscript. Standard formatting does not include inserting any photographs, graphics or images. See our formatting and design samples.

Custom Formatting - This is for those that want to use specialty fonts and custom layouts to correlate with the theme of the interior and genre. Custom formatting also includes the insertion of photographs, graphics, and images.

Enhanced Formatting - This is for authors that want to add a unique look to the interior of his or her book by using specialty fonts, images, and graphics that will provide a personal experience to the reader. This requires extensive formatting and many hands on hours, but the final outcome is a superb product that cannot be beat.

Interior Styles

Most new authors have difficulty in deciding on what text fonts to use. It becomes more confusing to an author if he or she searches the Internet to find what font to use for their book. Empire Publishing is here to help.

Classic, Traditional & Timeless: Option 3

Chapter One

CHAPTER TITLE

Book Title

BOOK SUBTITLE

Author Name

Kissing is the absolute best intimate experience there is, even more so than sex. Now that you have trenched your way through the muck of predators, losers, psychos, and liars, and you think you have finally found that rare diamond in the rough. You broke the ice with grace, wit, and charm. The first date was phenomenal, and there is a connection unlike anything you've experienced before. You get excited, your heart races with a mere thought of him or her. You think this could be the one, but wait, slow down there turbo. You haven't sealed the deal just yet. You have one crucial hurdle to get over, and that is, the frightening first kiss. No matter how good everything is prior to it, the first kiss could mean the beginning of a marvelous relationship or one of the biggest deal breakers there is. Delivering the perfect kiss can seal the deal on almost any new relationship, especially if the kiss is nothing short of epic.

Are you prepared for that fateful moment?

Timing is everything when it comes to that first kiss. Men are usually ready for it right out of the gate, but women require much more before allowing her mouth to be invaded.

1

Body Copy Font: Garamond   **Accent Font:** Palatino Linotype

Empire Publishing has created 10 templates for an author to simplify the search for a font that matches their content. We recommend reviewing each template on our website and choosing the option that best suits your book's genre and desired look and feel.

Interior Style Guide

Classic, Traditional and Timeless
Recommended genres: Literary Fiction and Memoir

Edgy, Bold and Unexpected
Recommended genres: Thriller, Mystery and Science Fiction

Modern, Clean and Contemporary
Recommended genres: Mind, Body and Spirit, Health and Wellness and General Nonfiction

Whimsical, Fun and Romantic
Recommended genres: Romance and Women's Literature

Template Style Guide Terms

Body Copy Font: The font used for the majority of a book's interior text.

Accent Font: A more decorative font used for headings and titles in a book. This font is best used in moderation, and can be a great tool to customize your book for your genre.

Visit
http://www.empire-publishing.com/empire/Interior_Options.html to view interior options.

Interior Layout and Design

There are a few self-service Print on Demand companies on the Internet that new authors may attempt to publish his or her book on their own. It sounds easy until they get into formatting the interior of their book properly to meet the printing guidelines of the printer. It can be rather frustrating when the book interior is rejected for improper formatting. Even if you do not decide to use Empire Publishing for all your publishing needs, we can still help you get your interior formatted correctly for printing and uploading a properly formatted manuscript.

Here's an example of what an author receives:

Up to 30 minute initial consultation with Graphic Designer to establish general book layout, graphic design and type faces.
Email consultation with designer
Creation of title page
Creation of copyright page
Creation of table of contents
Layout up to 352 pages of text with running heads and folios (page numbers) from your MS Word or WordPerfect document
Up to 10 photos
Up to 6 boxed text inserts per chapter
Up to 10 tables
Up to 20 bullet lists
Up to 20 additional photos, call-outs or bullet lists
Two levels of sub-heads
Basic Index

One PDF proof for proofreading
2 rounds of corrections (up to 50 corrections).
Final PDF proof for approval
Final PDF files for offset or digital printing
Complete PDF files on CD

Visit www.empire-publishing.com for details.

Line Spacing

Some authors prefer to use the single line spacing, but with certain fonts the interior will appear to be bunched up and can be difficult to read where the reader can easily lose their place within a paragraph. Depending on the font, it is recommended that you set your line spaces at 1.5 lines or 15pt.

Fonts

Using embedded fonts is not a problem, for print books or the digital formats that support the device display (Kindle Fire, ePUB formats, iBooks, NookColor, etc.), as long as the fonts are licensed. The Kindle devices display a single (default) font, called "Caecilia," which is essentially a Times New Roman clone. Some Kindle models allow the user to choose from six different font styles and sizes.

Most new authors have difficulty in deciding on what text fonts to use. It gets even more confusing to an author if he or she searches the Internet to find what font to use for their book.

The most used fonts used in printed books are:

Times New Roman
Garamond
Bookman Old Style
Book Antiqua
Fonts must be chosen for readability (legibility and easy on the eyes). Readers will not be happy if they experience eye strain due to a poorly chosen font.

Empire Publishing is here to help. We have created 10 templates for an author to simplify the search for a font that matches their content. We recommend reviewing each template and choosing the option that best suits your book's genre and desired look and feel.

Editing

An author must have his or her manuscript as polished as can be before publishing. Every writer knows this. Unfortunately, not everyone can afford to pay an editor $20 per page to edit his or her work, and editing your own work is almost impossible to do. Empire Publishing offers a professional editing service in our packages that are not going to break your bank account.

The best books from top authors released by major publishing houses have mistakes in them. This comes to one of the most dreadful aspects about going with a large publishing firm that no longer has proofreaders and one of the best aspects about publishing with print to order. There is no large costly inventory in stock and an error can be quickly rectified, even after a book is published. If you happen to find a mistake at a later date or need to make a change, those changes can be made within 48 hours.

Your manuscript must be as close to perfection as possible. If not, the overly abusive critics on Amazon will rip the book apart in reviews, and this will dramatically decrease sales. The reviews are so brutal on Amazon that authors are warned not to take them to heart. However, an author needs to avoid getting bad reviews in any way he or she can.

 If you want to publish a high-quality book, whether it is self-published or you are planning to go the old school route of attempting to secure an agent that might land you a contract with one of the large publishing houses, you must have your manuscript professionally edited.

Editing consists of:

• Typing errors / grammatical errors / misspellings.
• Consistency of style.
• Ambiguity and unclear meaning.
• Logical content and structure.
• Suitability for the intended audience.

Before publishing any book, it's wise to recruit a professional editor. It can be costly paying a freelance editor. If you cannot afford to do so, ask everyone, friends and family to read your book and take notes. Whereas you may think your book is polished after reading and editing yourself many times over, mistakes are bound to get past you. Authors tend to skip over errors because they know what they were trying to say. You need a second set of eyes to go over your manuscript. Do not rely on Microsoft Word to catch errors, in fact, MS Word, although a favorite of writers and most accepted within the industry, can also be an authors worst enemy. Its autocorrect features is known to make unwanted changes.

You can purchase Academic Literature software to help iron out the mistakes. However, there is not any flawless software available as of this date. Mistakes happen and are best corrected by a combination of organic (human) and mechanical software.

Empire Publishing performs two rounds of editing. First is mechanical with academic software and then personally done by editors with a College English Degree.

Most large book publishers will change the interior of your book to what they feel the story should say. They may even change the title of your book. Our editors will not change your manuscript, but will make recommendations for suggested corrections. The author receives these suggested edits via "Track Changes" in the original Microsoft Word file. We recommend submitting your manuscript as a Word 2007 Doc or older. It is your responsibility to accept or reject the editor's recommendations and make those changes to your manuscript. Our goal is not to alter your story or voice, but to enhance it for the better.

The estimated time frame for most manuscripts on an average is 4 weeks depending on length and complexity. Manuscripts with a lesser word count (60,000 words and under) are returned to the author quicker.

One of the "pros" with Printing on Demand (see next chapter) is if a mistake is found after publication it can easily be corrected within 24 hours. Only the books sold previously to the change, correction, addition or exclusion will have been printed as such. This gives an author piece of mind not having 10,000 plus books that contain a type-o that will drive him or her crazy.

Book Covers

Empire Publishing offers a wide range of options to authors for his or her cover designs. A book cover is more important than the contents of the interior. People are naturally drawn to looks and no matter what is inside a book, the cover will be what draws a potential buyers attention to it. To make matters worse, you have only eight seconds to grab his or her attention. The sad fact is that people really do judge a book by its cover. Empire Publishing designers have over 30 years experience in advertising design and layout with extensive knowledge of color theory and have worked with major companies such as Disney and Paramount Pictures. With so much competition, especially on Amazon and Barnes & Noble, it's extremely important to make your book cover stand out in a crowd.

Original Cover Art

There are many ways covers for books are designed. The cheapest route is using a pre-designed basic template, which is also the most common used for self publishing. Next is computer generated graphic covers. Then there is custom artwork specifically painted by an artist to best represent the content of the book. Empire Publishing offers them all. However, instead of paying $3,000 and up for an original piece of artwork, Empire Publishing has you covered and is one of the only publishers that have in house artists. Not only do authors get a unique cover but also receive the original artwork suitable for framing.

Premium Book Covers

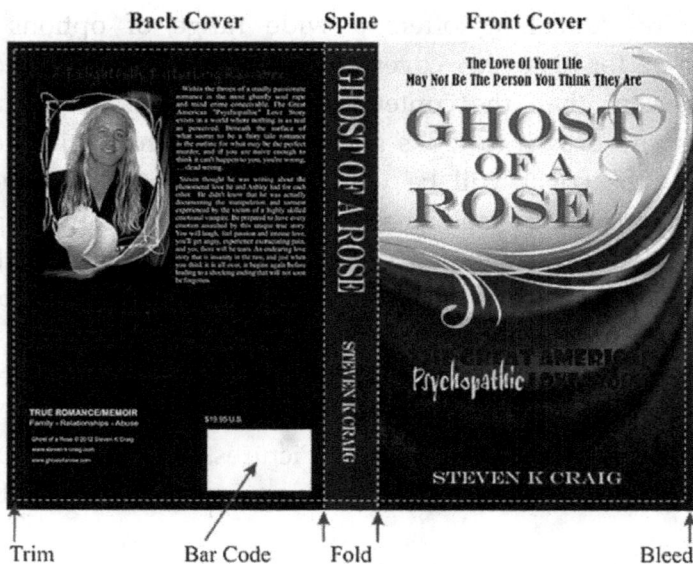

Give your book every opportunity to shine with our extensive design service. Our professional design team-working in collaboration with you-will create a highly engaging book cover that conveys your book's unique theme and messages. Your cover will include up to three images (depending on package), plus complementary colors, typography and other design elements.

An exceptional cover is a must for any book. Empire Publishing designs only top notch book covers. You can use any image of your own or we will provide on for you that fits your specifications. The majority of publishers that you are viewing online that design book covers are charging for just the cover. Ours includes the spine and back cover. The back cover is almost as important as the front because there is where your sales pitch (synopsis) must be. We assist you in creating the perfect back cover for you book.

Book covers for digital readers such as the Kindle, Nook, and Apple iPad need to be formatted at a required dimension that varies from the printed book cover. For some digital readers, the resolution must be much higher than that of a printed book. Empire Publishing includes a cover for digital readers that meet the requirements with the Premium Book Cover Package.

Budget Book Covers

Don't let the word "budget" mislead you. These are high quality book covers at a low price that come with both print and digital versions. The reason they are less expensive is that the working time is cut down by using one of our affiliates that produce high quality book cover designs. Avoid using simplistic cookie-cutter designs offered by many of the on-line indie publishers. Those type of covers will do no justice for you hard work as a writer and get overlooked by buyers.

Empire Publishing works with several companies that specialize in pre-designed book covers. There are thousands of covers to choose from to fit most genres. When a pre-designed cover is purchased, it becomes unavailable for use by any other author and is removed from the catalog. This package comes free with the Copper, Silver and Gold Print Combo Publishing Package. Also available on selected Digital Only publishing packages.

Free Book Covers

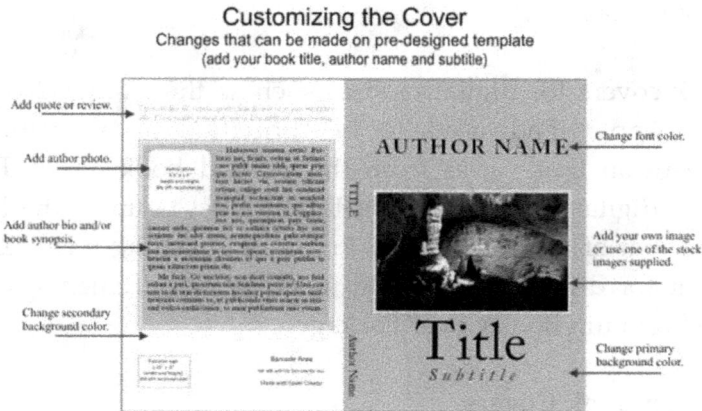

Customizing the Cover
Changes that can be made on pre-designed template
(add your book title, author name and subtitle)

Pre-designed and customizable book covers. These are only available with the Print and Digital Combo Publishing Packages. This service can be used with all the Print

Publishing Packages but is mainly used for the Bronze and Copper Combo Packages. You have your choice of gloss or matte finish.

Empire Publishing makes it easy for you. Simply choose you cover layout and then pick the desired colors for the fonts and backgrounds from the color chart. We will send you 6 different designs and color combinations based on your chosen template.

If you chose to supply your own front cover image and an author photo, you will be required to send Empire Publishing images no smaller than 300 dpi. Images below 300 dpi may print distorted. Do you need a royalty free image for your cover? Empire Publishing is here to help.

Our professional designers will develop a book cover featuring a single image and the template you selected. One round of revisions on any design element, other than the image, is included.

Book covers are available with either a gloss or matte finish.

Print on Demand

The publishing industry is rapidly changing, and the current trend is obviously the handheld electronic devices such as the Kindle and Nook. However, forty percent of avid readers still prefer the printed book over digital.

The problem with the way publishing has been done in the past is inventory. When a book is released a number of copies are printed on the first run. If the book does not do well in sales, the publishing company loses money, and when that happens, an author has little chance of getting a second book published.

Most Indie-Publishers will require an author to purchase up to 500 books upon publication. By using our printers, you are not required to purchase a single book. Print on Demand is the future of publishing. There is no costly inventory and no out of pocket expense for the author. It's simple, a buyer orders your book and it is delivered to his or her doorstep usually within 4 days.

As the author, you can purchase your book at a substantially lower cost and resell your book to make an even higher profit.

The power of on-demand printing and distribution-on-demand can make your book accessible for unlimited wholesale availability via the most sales channels in the industry.

Your book is printed on-demand, after a customer orders, using the latest digital printing technology available. With Empire Publishing your book's interior will be produced in full-color or black and white, depending upon the option you have selected. All book covers are printed in full color on cover stock and finished with a protective laminate-coating in your choice of either matte or glossy finish.

When we use the term "paperback", do not be mislead into believing that Empire Publishing produces those typically mass-marketed pocket books found in grocery stores. Paperback is the most widely used term for a non-hardcover, but our Trade paperback books are high quality "soft cover" books suitable for the top shelf in any bookstore. Your book is printed on high quality paper and will rival any produced by traditional publishing corporations. Every new author dreams of a hardcover version but in reality, they are extremely costly and dramatically reduce your profit margin. Our goal is to help you make money as a writer and not sell you an overpriced service.

Your book's interior will be produced in full-color or black and white, depending upon the option you have selected. All book covers are printed in full-color on cover stock and finished with a protective laminate-coating.

Covers are printed on 10pt stock in full-color and laminated for durability.

Our books are library-quality.

Professional trade paperback binding ensures a book to be proud of.

Books are printed to meet demand, so you benefit from inventory freedom.

ISBN

What's an ISBN?

An ISBN, or International Standard Book Number, is a unique 10- or 13-digit number assigned to every published book. An ISBN identifies a title's edition, publisher, and physical properties such as trim size, page count, and binding type. ISBN's are required for all published work.

How are ISBN's used?

Bookstores, retailers, and libraries identify books by their ISBNs. We print an ISBN barcode on the lower back right corner of every book we manufacture.

If you are self-publishing, we need to answer the most asked question about ISBN numbers, which is "Am I locked into not being able to re-release my book if I am offered a publishing contract by another publisher?" The answer is, "No you are not." Worst case scenario is all you may be required to do is change the title of your book. No changes to the interior would need to be made.

You have three ISBN options: you can either use an Assigned ISBN through a publisher such as Empire Publishing (free), a Custom Universal ISBN, or you can use your own ISBN purchased through Bowker®.

What are your ISBN options?

One concern new authors have is ownership of their book once an ISBN number is assigned. The question arises, "If I self publish can I still peruse a publishing contract with a

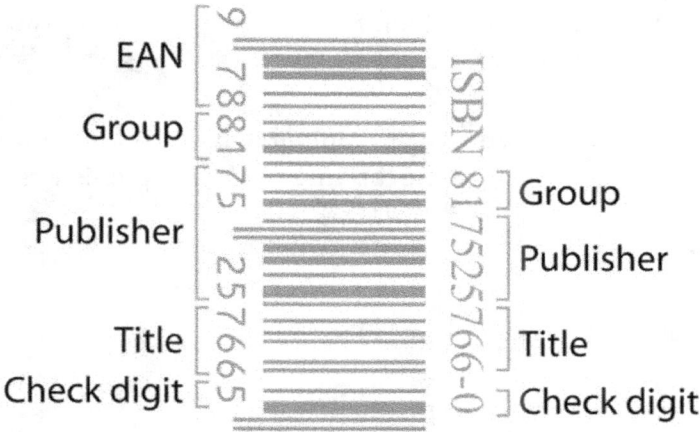

EAN
Group
Publisher
Title
Check digit

9 788175 257665

ISBN 8175257766-0

Group
Publisher
Title
Check digit

large publishing house? Even though agents will tell you that a publisher will reject anything previously self-published, that is not true. Take 50 Shades of Grey for example, which was originally self-published.

The real question is why wait many years hoping to gain a publishing contract when you can start promoting and making money right now? If a publisher decides to pick up your book, all they will do is request a title change and assign a new ISBN number. Self-publishing also allows you to do the same, for whatever reason, at any given time if you choose.

Publishers

When searching for a publisher you need to know a few things to look for. Quite a few publishers use the same printing companies so look for price variations in printing costs and royalties.

For example, here is a comparison between Empire Publishing and one of the top Internet based publishers.

Competitor:
6 x 9 - 460 Pages
Retail Price - $22.95
Royalty - $2.52
Author Discount price per book - $11.47
Empire Publishing:
6 x 9 - 460 Pages
Retail Price $19.95
Royalty $5.58
eStore* Royalty $9.57
Author Discount price per book $6.39

*The eStore is a direct link to an Internet page to sell your book Print on Demand/Publisher Direct.

Many publishers add fluff to their packages so it seems as if you are getting more than you actually are for what you spend. Also, most are using the same distributors. None are actually offering more than the next in basic distribution.

No longer do authors need to deal with the constant rejection of traditional publishers or the struggle, and more often than not, failure of self-publishing. Empire Publishing has incorporated the best of both worlds. And better yet is that you are in complete control and have full ownership of everything. Empire Publishing has one goal, and that is to lead the Independent Publishing Industry. We have spent countless hours researching the competing publishers to assemble the absolute best publishing packages to offer authors on every level. Empire Publishing now offers more publishing packages than anyone that range from Free Publishing and Budget Publishing to multiple levels of High End Publishing. We have created a Publishing Package to meet any need and budget. Our packages are designed to help launch an author's career and not see their hard work never get off the ground.

Rights

Before deciding upon which publisher to use, check to see what happens to your rights as the author. Many publishers take possession of the rights to the literary work once it is published. You should never give up the rights to your work. With Empire Publishing, the author retains all rights to his or her work. You should own and have control of your hard work and not turn it over to a company that will dictate, control and takeover ownership. Empire Publishing ensures that your work remains yours.

Royalties

Right now, you are having dreams of success with a bestselling novel. It pains me to have to burst your bubble, but you are where so many others have been before. Realistically, even if you are able to obtain a contract with a large firm, all your hopes and dreams will quickly be crushed. You will be given a $1,000 to $3,000 advance. You will have to dump your advance into advertising because the publishing firm will not invest any money. In addition, by signing with that large publishing firm, you will have given up the rights to your book. They now own your work. A board of directors will dictate the final content of your interior, formatting, book cover, and price. They will have you rewrite your story until it becomes what they feel it should be. The company will print a small test run of approximately 10,000 copies, and if your book doesn't become an instant hit, that's it, game over. Your book gets canned, they own the rights, and there is nothing more you can do. If your book does happen to sell well, you will receive minimal royalty payments that almost make you feel as if you have been robbed. The publisher takes most of the money and your agent gets 15%. If your book is sold on Amazon, where they sell your book at a discounted rate, they also take a nice chunk of the royalty. Everyone in line has his or her hand in the pot. For all your hard work, you may end up only averaging less than a $1.30 per book. It is solely up to you to generate sales because they will not. Writing your book was the easy part, now you have to become the salesperson. You do 90% of the work and everyone else keeps most of the money. Therefore, you must ask yourself, "Then why would I even want to get published by a large well-known publishing house?" Unless you are an established well-known author, forget about making millions of dollars or even thousands for that matter by signing everything over to a publishing firm. When publishing with Empire Publishing, the author receive 100% of his or her royalties (excluding fees and percentages by retailers such as Amazon) and the author retains 100% ownership of the title/work. No royalty money passes through Empire Publishing. We set up your account so all royalties earned goes directly to the author.

Contracts

There is no need for an author to sign a publishing contract to get his or her book on the market and making money. Why would anyone want to hand over all the hard work that they poured their soul into to large publishing firm that keeps most of the money and takes control of the rights to your work? Empire is a publishing service bureau and does not require an author to sign a contract. The author owns the book, the rights to the work, and all royalties earned go directly to the author. It's your story and your work - so should be the money and rights to it. However, Empire Publishing's offers packages so any aspiring author can get published, and to do so, we have included publishing packages that require no out of pocket expense to the author. Those packages do require a contract because Empire Publishing earns a percentage of the book sales on those programs. The best part is that our contact is a simple agreement that doesn't contain a bunch of legal lingo that needs a lawyer to interpret. Empire

Publishing does offer Traditional Publishing to specific authors of its choosing.

Distribution

Most online based publishers display a long list of distributors to draw in a potential customer which they claim every book will be available through if published with them. Again, this is fluff added for the naive. To begin with, even with the backing of a big name publisher, it is still at the bookstore's discretion whether to shelve the book or not. It is true that they have more clout to get a book into a retail store, but a self-published book is still available to the stores depending on which publisher the author chooses. As a literary service bureau, Empire Publishing is able to set up distribution for books with distributors that actually generate sales for books.

Standard Distribution

Amazon.com
Your book will be available to millions of customers on Amazon.com. Amazon is now the largest book retailer in the world.

Amazon Europe
Broaden your book's availability on Amazon's European websites including Amazon.co.uk, Amazon.de, Amazon.es, Amazon.fr, Amazon.it. Customers ordering from Amazon's European websites can take advantage of Free Super Saver Shipping, One-Day Shipping, 1-Click ordering, and Amazon Prime on eligible orders.

Empire Publishing eStore

Sell your book directly from your eStore. We'll handle the cart, credit card processing, and fulfillment of your customer's orders.

Wholesale Distribution

Authors receive worldwide wholesale distribution through major wholesalers. Your book is available for order through over 25,000 sales channels worldwide.

Expanded Distribution

Expanded Distribution offers you the opportunity to access a larger audience through more online retailers, bookstores, libraries, academic institutions, and distributors within the United States. Expanded Distribution will also improve discoverability of your book across all the channels.

Most online retailers, bookstores, and libraries find books through purchasing relationships with large distributors. If your book is not listed with these distributors, some retailers may not be able to buy your book, even if a customer specifically requests your title. Through Expanded Distribution you can distribute and make your title available for order (this does not guarantee that your book will actually be ordered) through the following channels:

Bookstores and Online Retailers - make your book available to online and offline retailers such as Barnes & Noble and to distributors such as Ingram and NACSCORP.

Libraries and Academic Institutions - make your book available through Baker & Taylor to libraries and academic institutions.

Smashwords Distribution

Smashwords is the world's largest distributor of indie ebooks and distributes to the world's largest ebook retailers. Over 70,000 serious writers and independent publishers publish and distribute with Smashwords. Many Smashwords authors have been previously published in print through mainstream publishers, or have had their works published in well-respected literary journals. A primary mission at Smashwords is to help make publishing more rewarding for the world's indie authors and more affordable to the world's readers. Authors and publishers earn 85% or more of the net proceeds from the sale of their works. Net proceeds to author = (sales price minus PayPal payment processing fees)*.85 for sales at Smashwords retail operation. Authors receive 70.5% for affiliate sales. Smashwords distributes books to most of the major retailers, including Apple iBooks, Sony, Kobo, Diesel, Page Foundry, Overdrive, Flipkart, Oyster, and Scribd. Sales originated by retailers earn authors/publishers 60% of the list price. To put these high royalty rates in perspective, it means if an author has a book they might otherwise publish via a traditional commercial publisher as a $8.00 mass market paperback, which would earn a 40 cent royalty, they could publish the same book at Smashwords as an ebook and earn up to $6.45 or 16 times more. Or, they could price their ebook on Smashwords for $3.99 and make nearly 8 times the per unit amount compared to selling a traditionally published print book.

There are no hidden fees. Smashwords gets a small commission on all net sales. Their commission is 10% of the retail price for sales through our retail distribution network (Apple, Barnes & Noble, Sony, Kobo, etc.) and library distribution network (Baker & Taylor Axis360, 3M Cloud Library, and others coming) and at the Smashwords store, 15% of the net for sales or 18.5% for sales that are originated by affiliate marketers.

Smashwords turns traditional authorship, publishing and pricing models upside down. With 85% of the net purchase price going to the author/publisher, author/publishers can charge readers significantly less for their works than would otherwise be possible through traditional print channels, while making greater per-unit profit on each book. When costs to the reader drop, there is a fundamental change to the demand side of the equation. This creates a virtuous cycle of more per-unit profit for the author/publisher, lower prices for consumers, and greater demand and consumption for written works. It's a win-win for authors and readers.

The best part is that there is no exclusive contract. They are solely a distributor. However, to publish an ebook with Smashwords it requires extensive formatting of the ebook that takes many hours to accomplish. If not done correctly, the book will be rejected repeatedly. This is where we come in to help.

Kindle

Amazon's Kindle is undoubtedly the number one electronic device used for digital publishing by authors and readers alike. However, Amazon has been making an attempt at monopolizing the digital publishing industry. They have done so by offering services that appear appealing to an author who assumes these expansions generate book sales. But do they? Not in the long run.

Amazon requires the author to agree not release his or her title on any other device, such as Barnes & Nobles "Nook" for a period of 90 days. An author is virtually forced into making the agreement so he or she can use other features offered by Amazon such as KDP Select, Kindle Countdown Deals, Kindle Unlimited, Kindle Owners' Lending Library and Free Book Promotion which all dramatically reduce the author's royalties.

These features work well when initially launching a new title and should be utilized by authors at the time of release. However, as time goes on, an author will lose a substantial amount of sales by remaining in agreement with Kindle and not publishing on the other devices. A word of precaution, an author must manually go to his or her Kindle Dashboard and uncheck the agreement or it will automatically renew every 90 days. An author can go back and re-enroll in the program at his or her discretion, but if Amazon catches the book published elsewhere during the 90 days, they will permanently disable that feature for future use.

Google Books/Play

Google Books is quickly becoming the world's largest eBookstore. Don't lose out on valuable book sales.

Drive Book Sales

Clicking on your book from a search results page takes users to a limited preview of your title – just enough to give them a taste of the book, as if they were browsing in a bookstore or library.

Links to bookstores and online retailers make it easy for users to go from browsing to buying. If you sell your books directly from your own website, your site receives "top billing," appearing first in the list of purchase links. Google Books previews also appear on book-related sites like online retailers and social book networks.

Increase awareness of your book
Reach Google's worldwide user base
Refer qualified traffic to your website
Help Users Find Your Books

Empire Publishing will add your title to Google's index. By matching the content in your books with user searches, Google Books connects your books with the users who are most interested in buying them.

Each Google Books result will display the book's title and author, a short excerpt containing the highlighted search terms, and other public data about the book.

Inserting Your Book on Google and Google Play

Find new fans and sell more books. Google Play reaches billions of readers around the world. One billion Android users, over 50 countries, and multiple platforms. When you sell books on Google Play, you reach readers you never thought possible. Empire Publishing properly formats your eBook to Google Books requirements, uploads your files, publishes and sets up your account to receive royalties directly from Google for Google Play.

Enhance Your Preview Page

As a Google Books partner, you have access to Google Preview - code that allows you to embed previews of your books right on your website. With Google Preview, you can easily enhance your site.

Visitors to your site can browse and search within your books right on each book's product page.

Track Your Success
Of course you'll want to track how you're doing—and you can. Online reports let you manage your account information, view how many consumers have looked at your titles, see click rates on purchase links, and review other stats related to the Google Books program. You can customize reports to view results by date, title or ISBN.

Apple iPad and iPhone

If you've shopped around for a publisher, you have probably seen many of them offering the service of getting your book published on Apple's iBooks for the iPad and iPhone for around $699.00. Don't waste your money. Apple has tried to monopolize on their service by requiring both authors and readers to own Apple devices. There is no need for this nor spending a ridiculous amount of money to be published directly with Apples iBooks. Not to mention, iBooks sales are not the best out there and it may take a long time to recoup that large investment. However, you do want your book available on every reading device on the market. We've got your back and have you covered.

Use our Smashwords Publishing and Distribution Service which is by far less expensive, and your book will not only be available on iBooks, it will also be available on Sony Reader, Kobo and the Diesel eBook Store.

Barnes & Noble

Print - With limited shelf space, an independently published book will most likely not be available in the retail stores. However, the title becomes available online at Barnes & Noble's website and goes into their computer system so it can be ordered at any of the retail outlets. This in no means does it rule out getting an independently published book into a retail store. It can be done.

Digital - The "Nook" from Barnes & Noble is the second leading digital reader on the market and one an author should not overlook. Authors need to make their books available on as many devices as possible to gain maximum sales potential. Not doing so will limit the potential audience and drastically hamper book sales. Only books that have been submitted via the required process and format are available for NOOK readers to purchase and enjoy. The Nook has a fantastic free reading app to download that allows readers to sync their account to other devices such as smartphones, tablets and computers. A reader can change devices and pick up where they last read. Get your book in the hands of millions of potential readers worldwide. When ordering select combo-publishing packages from Empire Publishing a book will be formatted and published on Barnes & Noble's Nook.

Personal Marketing Assistant

Whomever you publish with it's wise to hire a personal marketing assistant. The failure of most authors is due to not having a marketing plan. In order to generate book sales, an author platform must be developed. However, many authors get lost, don't have the personal time to dedicate for marketing or simply just don't know where and how to build a solid platform. There is no secret formula or a plan that works for every author. Most occasions it takes extensive research to locate the optimal area of marketing for potential book sales.

Every published author has a dream for success, but for most, it is almost an impossible dream because he or she cannot dedicate the required time due to having a day job and daily duties. To reach your writing goals, you must market your book and it will not do it on its own. This is where a marketing assistant can help. A personal marketing assistant can handle any and all details related to marketing your book.

How can an Empire Publishing Personal Marketing Assistant help you?

First of all, we assign one assistant to you that will stay with you throughout the service. The assistant will develop a Marketing Plan specifically for your book. He or she will do the research and fine tune a plan to target the audience best suited for your book. Your marketing assistant will develop a detailed marketing plan with suggested actions and other valuable information that will generate more book sales.

Your personal marketing assistant will help schedule books signing's in your area and coordinate every detail. Your assistant will put together an attention gathering press kit and submit it to media outlets such as print and radio for possible interviews.

Your marketing assistant will diligently work on developing a solid foundation for your author platform to support and market your writing. This includes websites and social media accounts. Any and all leads that are established will have follow ups performed by your Personal Assistant to ensure you reach each of them while they are interested.

Don't allow your hard work in writing fall short as so many authors have done in the past and still do today. Empire Publishing wants to see you be successful as a writer.

Author Representative

The time may come when an author needs help and guidance in your pursuit of becoming a bestselling author. Some publishing packages through Empire Publishing provide the author with a personal Author Representative. The assigned professional will be on hand whenever needed. The representative is available as a liaison between the author and outside companies for assistance in areas such as radio interviews, book signings and more. An author representative is only available with the Gold, Platinum, and Titanium Combo-Publishing packages, traditional publishing contracts, and Platinum eBook Publishing Package.

Marketing

As an author, you must also be an entrepreneur, a salesperson, a marketing specialist, and a public relations spokesperson. Your book is the product you are selling to public. Many first time authors think his or her book will automatically sell just by being on Amazon. Unfortunately, it will not. You need to promote your product every way you can. To generate sales, you need to network and be seen. There are many ways to do this and Empire Publishing is here to assist you. Most first time authors cut corners and go the cheap route by using Staples or worse yet, print from their computer. Handing out cheap promotional items is a bad reflection on your product. Empire Publishing offers premium quality promotional items at an affordable rate. The items and services we provide will separate you from those that don't take the business of being a writer seriously. There are many reasons some writers succeed and others do not. This is one of them because most authors don't go above and beyond to become successful.

Websites

The days of getting your book on a shelf in a large retail bookstore for shoppers to find are long gone. An author that is serious about success must have a personal website. It is an utmost necessity in building name recognition. Regardless of whether you get signed with an agent, a contract with a large publishing house or decide to self-publish, you need to promote your work yourself. In any case, to sell books, you must develop a solid platform.

With the lack of bookstores, and most shopping being done on the Internet, a strong web presence is mandatory to gain interest in your product and to generate book sales.

Don't be fooled into thinking a large publisher, as in one of the big five, will invest any money into advertising your work because they don't. In fact, most publishers will not talk to an author that doesn't already have a well designed website and established platform.

It is vital to have a web presence that is an integral part of your book marketing plan. A successful author uses every tool available to promote his or her work, and the greatest tool of all is the Internet. Without a personal website, you will never reach the full potential of book sales.

Several organizations offer plans for building a website for you, but be careful. Most of the companies offering to build your website will end up owning your domain name, and this has caused many people much grief after a year when his or her website mysteriously disappeared from the Internet.

One well know indie-publisher even cheapened their service by building websites for authors on Go-Daddy, only to drop the websites service which caused many authors to lose their website overnight without warning.

In order to be seen on the search engines, you must generate name recognition and have knowledge of SEO (Search Engine Optimization). It is impossible to achieve either by purchasing a cheap website or using a free service. Google tends to change their procedure and requirements for ranking a website higher on the search engine. Verification codes must be embedded into the header, pages must be indexed individually and correct meta-tags must be placed within each page. Also, the website should be "pushed" to the Google servers once a week. This means you need to manually submit for indexing and robotic web crawlers. On top of that, Google now requires rich content that is frequently updated and websites that cross link with other websites. It takes extensive work to gain a strong web presence.

We have seen publishers offer a website and even an e-store to the author, only to have them disappear after a year with no means of retrieving the website or domain name.

The publishers that offer a website (with a hidden built in fee) in their publishing packages are basically just a designated page on the Internet. These pages do little to nothing without SEO unless the author directs potential buyers to the page. Don't be fooled into believing otherwise.

Empire Publishing offers three website packages to fit anyone's need or budget. The author receives more than just an Internet page. When the job is complete, we never leave him or her high and dry. Updates and changes can be performed at any given time at the author's request.

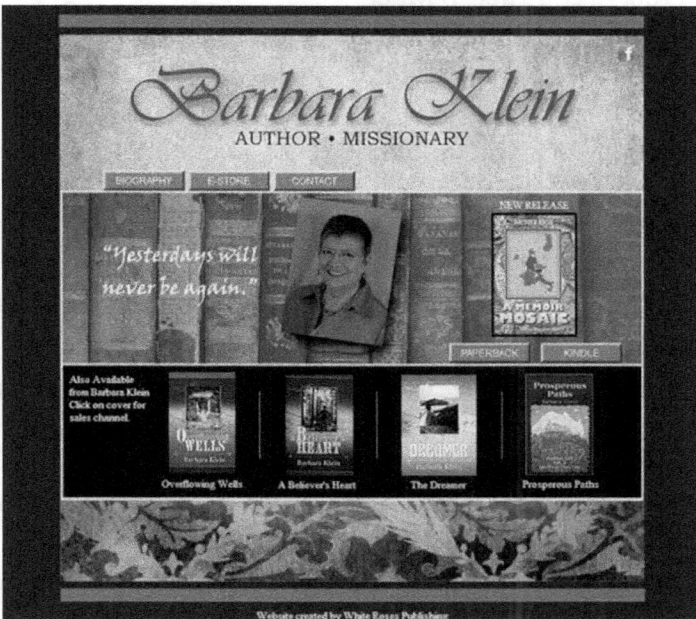

An author website through Empire Publishing has the options to include the following:

1) Custom Website Design
2) Author Biography Page
3) 24 Images/Scans
4) 4 Preview/Text Pages
5) Contact Page with Form
6) Order Page
7) Social Network Links
8) Book Review Page
9) Guest Book
10) Hit Counter
11) Integrated E-Store
12) Photo Gallery
13) Embed YouTube Widget
14) Subscriber Newsletter
15) E-Store/Shopping Cart
16) Blog Integration
17) Social Media Integration
18) 3 Month SEO
19) Custom HTML

With Empire Publishing you own and have full control over everything you do with Empire Publishing. Empire Publishing has over fifteen years experience in website development, meta-tags, and search engine optimization. We can build you a custom website that will integrate all your sales channels and social media outlets. If you don't know how to operate social media outlets such as Facebook, we can handle that for you as well, and create custom banners for your brand as an author. Authors can save money by choosing an Empire Publishing package that includes an author website. However, if you already have a book on the market, we can still build an author website for you.

Empire Publishing can build your website and we use our source/servers for hosting it. We can put together an attractive author website package with a built in blog, and many more add-on components at a surprisingly affordable price.

You retain complete ownership of your website and domain name. As with all our services, when we are finished, we had the keys over to you. You are the owner and in control. However, we never leave you hanging and will always be there to help. We even sent you the files your website and give you the information on what software to use just in case you want to take full control and update the website yourself in the future. No one does this!

Authors that use Empire Publishing receive a single-page website that can be used for promotion, sample, contact information, book synopsis and link where to purchase book. The web page includes an author bio and photo, plus the cover of his or her book. It does not include a registered domain name. The web address will have an Empire Publishing extension followed by the author name or book title. Example: www.empire-publishing.com/"your name or book title". An author webpage is included in the Silver and Gold Combo-Publishing Packages, and the Premium eBook Publishing Package.

As a way of helping authors even further, specific packages through Empire Publishing receive a feature listing in Empire Publishing's online bookstore. The book is listed in the appropriate category for its genre. Only Gold, Platinum and Titanium publishing appear on the front page and will be placed in two sections (genre listing and Empire Recommends).

Your book listing will include a cover image, synopsis and a link to purchase your book at the sales channel of your choosing (i.e. Amazon.com or your website).

The picture below is a sample of an Empire Publishing Bookstore page. It is another way of gaining name recognition on the Internet and used for Search Engine Optimization as well as web page and sales channel that contains all the information about an author and the book. The free page for specific publishing packages includes a unique ip address with author's name, publishing information, links to author's website and social media outlets, author bio, links to purchase book, embedded video trailer (does not include production of video), book overview, free preview, Facebook "share" and "like" button, and a twitter "share" button.

Electronic Press Kit

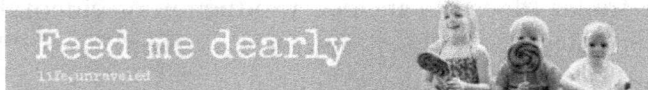

Feed me dearly
life, unraveled

AUTHOR: JESSICA FIORILLO

Media Kit 2013

About the author:
Jessica Fiorillo is the author behind "Feed me dearly", a food and lifestyle blog. She's also one of the contributors to Big City Moms, which reaches an audience of 300,000+ women.

With an MBA from Berkeley, an undergraduate degree in Psychology from Brown University, and nearly 10 years of experience as a brand strategist with industry leader Lippincott, she has a finely-tuned understanding of how brands can best position themselves, and how she can help support their mission.

About the blog:
"Feed me dearly" is the blog that she created in March, 2013 after realizing that cooking – and family life – are pleasures to be enjoyed, not endured, despite all of the challenges. She lives in New York City with her husband, three kids aged 2, 3, and 5, and 7-year old dog Jack, who's been able to weasel his way into more than his fair share of posts.

Contact details:
www.feedmedearly.com
feedmedearly@gmail.com
415-318-6152

- @feedmedearly
- Facebook.com/feedmedearly
- Instagram.com/feedmedearly
- Pinterest.com/feedmedearly

As featured in:
The Daily Meal POPSUGAR Moms

ELIZABETH st circle of moms

fresh20 Mommy page

About her audience:
- Primarily female, ages 25–45
- Has children or is expecting
- College educated
- Both stay at home and working parents

An electronic press kit is essentially a collection of digital documents (most commonly PDF files) which are packaged together and made available to download on your website and to send out via email. Empire Publishing will create an eye catching Electronic Press Kit for you.

Electronic Press Kits make it easier for media outlets to quickly and efficiently gather information about your book and about you as an author. Press kits are an excellent way to gain interest in your book and stand out above other authors vying for book sales. Purchase this kit and Empire will send you an email requesting what is needed to create your Press Kit before getting started.

What is in a Press Kit
Press kits are useful to everyone from musicians to artists, but as an author you will definitely need to include the

items listed below. We ask that you supply us with as much information as possible to create your Media Kit.

Author Biography
This should be written in third person and maintain a professional tone throughout. Don't let it drone on any longer than a single page and be sure to include a head shot to go with it.

Free Chapter of Your Book
A full sample chapter to your book that includes links to buy a complete copy on Amazon or wherever else you are selling it online.

Press Release
An engaging press release is to announce the publication of your book and spread the word initially.

Interview Q&A's
This can be example questions and your answers if you haven't actually been interviewed by anyone yet. If you have several, pick a couple of your strongest and do your best to highlight the most important parts of each one.

Sample Book Reviews

Plug a couple of the best online reviews for your book. If you do not have any reviews yet, we will write a few positive reviews for you to get you started.

Social Media

Investment in Social Media is a Necessity, Not a Luxury. Investing time and resources into a social media strategy to promote and sell your book is most definitely a necessity. As an author, you are a business and your book is the product you are marketing to the public. Businesses are coming to terms with the need to integrate their social media efforts with their content strategy, and are seeing the impact of social media in terms of lead generation, referral traffic, and revenue. Any author that is serious about selling his or her book knows that the social media outlets cannot be overlooked because they are a useful and powerful promotional tool.

The benefits of social media are many, but they include: Improved social signals (which are a factor in the search-ranking algorithm), Author (book) branding, Improved brand awareness, Word-of-mouth advertising, Increased customer loyalty and trust, Improved audience reach and influence. Social media is also one of the three pillars of SEO (search engine optimization to get your a higher ranking).

In order to sell books today, an author needs a strong web (internet) presence. Name recognition is a must, and the best way to accomplish that is having the authors name on the Internet in every place possible. This included utilizing every social media outlet which includes Facebook, Twitter, Pinterest, Tumblr, Google Plus, Linkedin, Youtube, Stumbled Upon, Wordpress, Blogger, AboutMe, and VK Europe. It takes a lot of work and is time consuming to build and maintain a variety of social media outlets. New content must be constantly added to hit the newsfeeds so the book/product is seen. Basic advertising practice is to imbed the product into the consumers mind.

Empire Publishing will set up all the social marketing accounts needed for you to get your book in the public eye and on the right path to selling your title to the proper target market. We make hassle and stress free for you, quickly, and easily. We create an attractive banner and cover photo with your book to incorporate with all your independent social media outlets and network them together.

A social media page needs to be set up and designed to attract people to it, and give them a desire to return. People will pass on by or not even look at it if the page is not attractive. The following list is what should be done to each page and is included in Empire Publishing's Social Media packages.

Custom Banner/Header
Author Photograph
Custom Background
Author Bio
Photo of Book Cover
Embed Youtube Video
Links to Book Estore and Website

Book Synopsis
Quotes/Reviews
Cross Link Social Media Networks

The social media packages that our competitors offer only contain 4 platforms, Facebook, Twitter, Linkedin, and Youtube. Empire Publishing's package utilizes 12 of the leading social media platforms to give your book maximum exposure.

Networking is a key to unlocking substantial sales. Authors should join every social media outlet and get involved in discussions. There are many pages dedicated to authors for self promotion. Take advantage of these pages to build a following. Seldom do readers seek out authors. Authors need to spend the time seeking the reader and inviting them to his or her page. Empire Publishing sends out invites to its fan base and directs them to a new author's page to help launch the author's page.

Web Banners

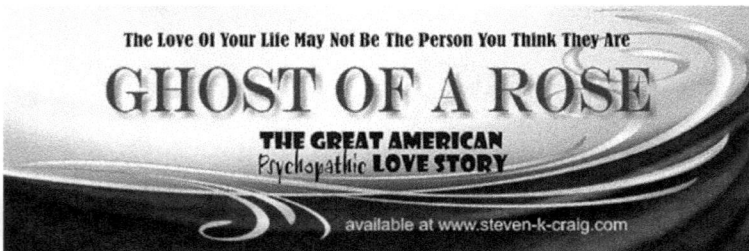

The Love Of Your Life May Not Be The Person You Think They Are

GHOST OF A ROSE

THE GREAT AMERICAN
Psychopathic LOVE STORY

available at www.steven-k-craig.com

When using the Social Media Networks to promote your book, you need a custom banner that is eye catching. Banners are almost as important as your book cover for attracting potential buyers. On an average, you have about 3 seconds to get the attention of someone browsing the Internet, so you need to be able to immediately grab his or her interest long enough to hold them there. Empire Publishing has in house graphic designers with over 30 years experience. Each social media network requires a different size banner. We send you the correct sizes for Facebook, Twitter, Tumblr, and Google+.

Facebook Advertising

Facebook is one of the leading power tools to promote and sell books. At one time, magazine ads were the way to go, but since the monthly print publications have dramatically dropped in sales and availability, the Internet has become the dominate marketplace. Facebook Advertising is the easiest way to target certain markets by age group, interests, and location. Strategically, this works well for an author to get his or her book seen by potential readers that have a specific interest in the topic of your book. It's the best bang for the buck. However, recent Facebook changes have made it more difficult to keep in touch with an audience and Empire Publishing's marketing department stays on top of the changes and adjusts the strategy to make sure you get maximum exposure. We perform the research for the author to find the core audience and then target them as the market. The author's book gets seen by those most likely to purchase it without wasting money on those that have no interest.

When an author uses Empire publishing to handle his or her Facebook advertising campaign, the author receives:

Sponsored Facebook Advertising
Custom Designed Advertisement
Paid Post "Boost" after 20 Days
Newsfeed Advertising
Improved Name Recognition

Goodreads Author Program

Networking is a major factor in books sales in today's world. The Goodreads Author Program is a feature designed to help authors reach their target audience — passionate readers. This is the perfect place for new and established authors to promote their books. Link to Facebook and invite your friends. Build an audience and fan base with avid readers.

Make your profile a dynamic destination for curious readers. Here are some of the features you can use on your profile:

- Add a picture and bio.
- Share your list of favorite books and recent reads with your fans!
- Write a blog and generate a band of followers.

- Publicize upcoming events, such as book signings and speaking engagements.
- Share book excerpts and other writing.
- Write a quiz about your book or a related topic.
- Post videos.
- Add the Goodreads Author widget to your personal website or blog to show off reviews of your books.

Promote Your Books

Get the word out! Here are some of the promotional tools available on Goodreads:

- Advertise your book to the Goodreads Community – 25 million readers!
- List a book giveaway to generate pre-launch buzz.
- Lead a Q&A discussion group for readers.
- Participate in discussions on your profile, in groups, and in the discussion forums for your books.

Empire Publishing can set up your account and build your profile. We insert your book and begin building your platform. Your book will be put on our bookshelf to be seen buy our readers and we will even send out invites to those that are interested in your book's genre. At that point the author can either take over the helm or we will update it once a month for him of her.

Amazon Author Exposure

Think of yourself as a company and your book is the product you are trying to get consumers to purchase. There is no magic wand to wave or hidden secrets regardless of the number of those being peddled to new authors. As with any business, to achieve sales, you must advertise your product. In today's world, the Internet is one of the best advertising tools available. However, much work needs to be done to get your book seen by consumers. Selling books on Amazon.com is a numbers game that is won by building name recognition and climbing the ranking system. The more exposure an author has on the Internet, the more name recognition on search engines and the higher the ranking, which means more in book sales. This is achieved by building a strong author platform. Without it, an author will only achieve minimal books sales, if any at all. Getting your book listed on Amazon.com does not mean it will sell. In fact, this way of thinking is where many authors fail. We may not like it, but this is the way the publishing industry operates, and we can expect more changes in the future. Improve your book visibility and ranking on Amazon.com by including the Amazon Exposure Program. Competing publishers are offering this service for $699. As with all of our services, we aim to beat their prices and offer more for far less out of pocket expense.

When Empire Publishing sets up an Amazon Author Exposure page the author receives:

Create Author Central account.

Author Profile Photograph and Biography.
List of author books and links to Amazon.com.
Multi-Media/Photo Inclusion.
Author blog feed integration.
Author Twitter feed integration.
Book trailer insertion.
Amazon book sales report.
Sales by geography map
Author rank history on Amazon.
Add author events.
Author discussion forum.
3 Amazon Collections Boards featuring your book
w/unique keywords.
Link to Author Website.
Author e-mail address inclusion.

Shelfari

Shelfari promotes its "virtual bookshelf" as one of its main features. The virtual bookshelf displays covers of books which the user has entered, with popups to show the user's book information (review, rating, and tags). Sorting by author, title, date, rating, or review is available to the viewer of the shelf. Users may organize books into different shelves, including already read, currently reading, planning to read, wish list, currently owned, and favorites.

The Shelfari catalog may be edited by users, though some changes must be approved by Shelfari "librarians." Using wiki functionality users may edit each book's authors, title, publication data, table of contents, first sentence, and series. Users may also combine redundant books into a single entry or add new titles not found in the catalog. Similar to books, author pages may be edited or created. In addition to general catalog maintenance, users are encouraged to contribute reviews, descriptions, lists of characters and settings, author biographies, categories, and descriptive tags.

Most books in the Shelfari catalog come from the large Amazon catalog, including Amazon Marketplace listings added by independent resellers. These books link back to Amazon and display current pricing and links to AbeBooks for used book sales.

Shelfari has a group creator, which allows you to talk, play, or discuss your books.

Book Daily

Guaranteed Exposure to 50,000 Readers and Potential Buyers in 30 Days. BookDaily makes it easy for readers to discover new books and new authors. Join the growing community of authors who use BookDaily as a tool in developing their online promotional strategies. Not that long ago, an author would do a book tour for a new release by travelling to bookstores. That's not the case anymore with bookstores toppling like dominos. Today an author tours his or her book by utilizing the Internet. When it comes to book sales, it doesn't matter how good your book is if new readers can't find it! According to Publishers

Weekly, a staggering 764,448 self-published titles were produced in 2009 and has seen a growth of 58% since then. How will you ever break through that clutter? Let us do the legwork and start your book tour on BookDaily with a simple and affordable author promotion.

BookDaily Marketing Benefits:

Post the first chapter of a book for readers to preview and review.
Post author biography and photo.
Include a link to author's website or blog for new traffic and SEO value.
Upload Youtube book video trailer.
Receive a regular author marketing newsletter from leaders in digital book marketing.
Promote a book with a BookDaily free widget, press release information and more.

Book Daily Featured Author:

BookDaily distributes a book to at least 50,000 readers and their companion website ArcaMax.com by email. These active subscribers expect to receive newsletters and book chapters from BookDaily each day. Typically 5000 or more open and read their daily email from BookDaily. A book title will also receive featured placement during the month on BookDaily and ArcaMax, driving additional exposure and readership.

Empire Publishing sets up an author's account and builds his or her profile. We insert a sample chapter, links and build the authors platform. When Empire Publishing has completed building the authors profile and launched the promotional campaign, we hand the keys over to the author so he or she has full control of the account. At any given time, the author can come back and Empire

Publishing will perform updates and run further promotion campaigns.

Video Marketing

An author must use every resource available to him or her when promoting a book. Many new authors assume that once his or her book is available on Amazon that it will sell itself. That way of thinking couldn't be any further from the truth. An author needs to hustle, regardless of which publisher produces the book or else all his or her hard work will be for nothing, except having books that they worked hard to write and get published do little more than sit on a shelf collecting dust. We want you to go much further than that and be successful as an author.

Face it, the Internet is the best tool for promoting a book, and to benefit from it, you must build name recognition. The more your name is spread across the Internet, the higher you climb on the search engines, which in turn, exposes your book to a larger audience. All successful authors know this and use it to its full advantage. Videos are one of the best steps in going viral to large audience. A video teaser/trailer demands, "Look at me!"

Producing a video teaser/trailer is a complicated process. Our production team assembles the concept, theme, graphics, transitions, and effects. They incorporate your book cover, profile picture, snippets, hook-lines, background music, and do voice-over's. You get a video that proudly represents you, the author, and your literary masterpiece. We make it easy for you by uploading your video to YouTube where it can be distributed by linking or embedding into all the social media platforms. We even do that for you as well. Add a book trailer to your personal website and post it on your blog. Your video will be uploaded to the Empire Publishing YouTube channel and made available for the author to use anywhere he or she chooses.

You receive a completed video book trailer in three different 16:9 aspect ratio formats:

1280 x 720 QuickTime MOV file
1280 x 720 MPEG4 file
1280 x 720 WMV file

If you choose to make your own video trailer, try to keep it around 60 seconds and focus on the selling points of the story and using your hook-lines. Also, include information on where to purchase your book. Don't assume they will search for it on Google or Amazon. Depending on the complexity of the book interior, some can go up to 5 minutes. View a sample book trailer at https://www.youtube.com/watch?v=blf3xPi-6pc

Audio Excerpt

There are many uses for an audio excerpt from a book. Not to mention, an audio excerpt can make an author stand out above of all others vying for book sales. Potential book buyers will be attracted to a book they can hear it.

However, reading a chapter into a Smartphone to record it will not suffice. Professional recording and editing equipment must be used.

Empire Publishing offers a package that comes with a professionally recorded audio excerpt from your book and can include music and sound effects to enhance the listening experience. The audio is limited to 600 words from the author's book. You have the choice of either having it sent to you in an MP3 format via email or one a compact disk. Empire Publishing's audio excerpt includes a free uploaded to Youtube.

Celebrity Endorsements

Empire Publishing prides itself on not taking advantage of authors by trying to sell a service that is bogus. Several publishers on the Internet offer "Celebrity Endorsements" as a service for a fee over $100. However, there is a catch to it. They don't actually put you in direct contact with any celebrity. What they do is send you an address that may or may not be current for the celebs. You can obtain address on your own from the same place these publishers do for much less. Go to   www.imdb.com   (internet movie database). Sign up for IMDbPRO. It only cost $15.95 per month and you can cancel at any time. IMDb is the largest celebrity database on the Internet, and there you will be able to find the celebrity contact addresses that you are looking for, including the celebs, including his or her agent and production company. As a Empire Publishing author, we will show you how to be successful obtaining a celebrity endorsement.

Pro Photo Shoot

With thousands of new authors emerging on a monthly basis, all of whom are battling for attention to his or her literary work, you need to go further than everyone else in marketing aspects. Stand out above the others with a professionally staged photo shoot that can be used in a

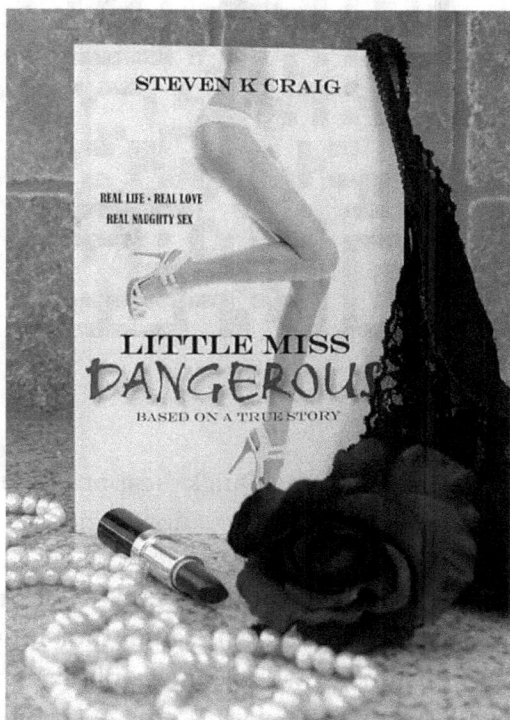

multitude of ways for promotion. Success with Internet marketing is producing an array of eye catching imagery.

Empire Publishing has in house photographers and stagers that produce high quality imagery to enhance the appeal of any book. The photo's can be used for print and digital advertising, blog posts, social media presentations, posters, banners and fliers.

QR Codes

QR code (abbreviated from Quick Response Code) is the future in advertising that is here now. The QR Code has become a focus of advertising strategy, since it provides quick and effortless access to the brand's website or sales channel. The QR Code will assist an author in generating book sales as consumers with a camera phone can scan the image of the QR Code to open a web page (author website)

in the telephone's browser without any delay. QR Codes benefit an author by placing it on any form of advertising such as fliers, sell sheets, posters, and banners. It has been proven that consumers will only view an advertisement for 3 seconds and then move onto something else. Within those 3 seconds, the potential buyer can snap a picture of your QR Code, save in a folder, and come back to it later to spend more time looking into the author's product. It's a fast paced world and an author needs to use every advantage available. Empire Publishing will create your personal QR Code and imprint it on any of the other paid marketing services you choose to do with us.

Place QR Code on any item.   Scan with any Smart Phone.   Instantly goes to Website
(free app)   (sales channel)

Media Networks such as Facebook, they have specific guidelines which we will set up your advertisement to comply with those guidelines.

Print Advertising

Getting in the public eye with printed promotional tools is a tried and true way generating sales. Word of mouth is still one of the best sales tools, but it needs help to get it rolling. Most first time authors cut corners and go the cheap route by using Staples or worse yet, print from their computer. Handing out cheap promotional items is a bad reflection on your product. Empire Publishing offers premium quality promotional items at an affordable rate.

The items and services Empire Publishing provide will separate you from those that don't take the business of being a writer seriously. There are many reasons some writers succeed and others do not. This is one of them because most authors don't go above and beyond to become successful. Empire Publishing offers a variety of high quality printing services.

Business Cards

Business cards are a must for any business. However, you want your cards to have the look of being professionally done. Business cards printed from your computer or low budget printing look cheap and are cheap. That is not the impression you want to give a potential buyer. It will reflect poorly upon the product you are trying to sell, which is your book.

Sell Sheets

Sell Sheets are what many authors use to get his or her book into retail stores. Our premium sell sheets are designed to grab the buyer's attention. It contains the sales pitch, book cover, synopsis, book data, publishing information, contact info, and we include a free QR Code for the retail store buyer to scan for ordering your book.

Bookmarks

Bookmarks are a useful promotional tool. Unlike business cards, they will not be lost in a wallet. Bookmarks almost never get thrown out and always get used. In turn, your bookmark will be seen repeatedly by a potential customer and will increase your book sales. There are many uses for a bookmark in promoting your book other than its intended use. Some authors have been known to go into a bookstore and insert their bookmarks into bestselling books in the same genre as their own. Sneaky, but it works.

Postcards

Postcards are a highly effective and efficient way to reach people. Empire Publishing's 15PT Card stock is our standard paper stock which is ideal for postcard mailers, handouts, and flyers. Our premium postcards are a high-quality presentation of your cover, and contain your book and ordering information on the back side. These are a fantastic way to generate interest and most bookstores will allow you to leave them on a counter.

Multi-Media

Most authors cannot afford paid advertisements in magazines, but we make them available for use in many media forms, including the Internet and social media outlets. Potential buyers skip over ads that have been used repeatedly. To sell books, an author needs to continually bombard the Internet with fresh and attractive advertisements. Empire Publishing can keep you in the public eye and generate interest in your book with colorful new ads whenever you need the change.

The graphic designers at Empire Publishing have over 30 years experience with graphic design, layout and printing for companies such as Disney Pictures, Republic Pictures, Paramount Pictures, and Rhino Records. Empire Publishing will create an advertisement for your book to use as promotion in print or digitally on the Internet that will be appealing to potential buyers. If you plan on

The graphic designers at Empire Publishing have over 30 years experience with graphic design, layout and printing for companies such as Disney Pictures, Republic Pictures, Paramount Pictures, and Rhino Records. Empire Publishing will create an advertisement for your book to use as promotion in print or digitally on the Internet that will be appealing to potential buyers. If you plan on advertising with Social Media networks such as Facebook whom have specific guidelines which we will set up your advertisement to comply with those guidelines.

A Beautifully Disturbing Romance
Based On A True Story

Within the throes of a madly passionate romance is the most ghastly soul rape and mind crime conceivable. Illusion and manipulation are used to create the Perfect Murder.

The Love Of Your Life
May Not Be The Person You Think They Are

GHOST OF A ROSE

Psychopathic

STEVEN K CRAIG

Available December 2012
Amazon.com ISBN-13: 978-1481015554

Author
Steven K Craig

www.ghostofarose.com

Posters

Posters are an excellent way to be seen. Make your presence known by adding color to your booth, hand out the posters as promotional gifts, and sign them for fans. You must promote to generate sales. Not to mention, these high quality posters would look great framed and hanging in your house or office.

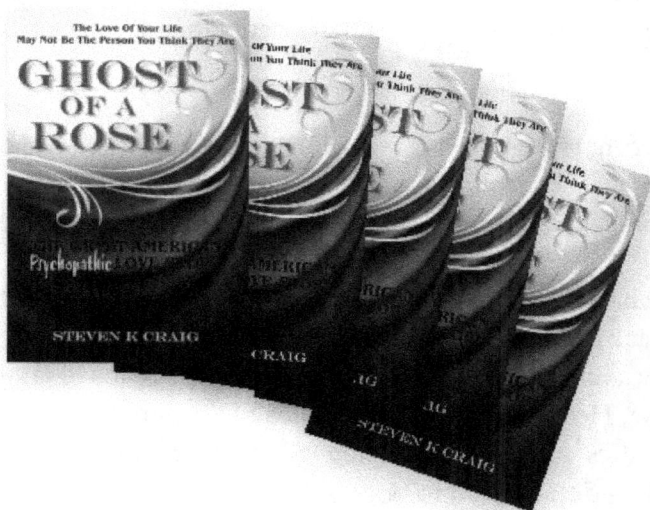

Large Posters include the book cover in full color. Our designers will create a visually striking layout that best represents your book.

Large Posters - Trim Size: 24" x 36"
Small Posters - Trim Size: 11" x 17"

Book Reviews

Not too long ago, newly released books generated sales by being displayed on tables for patrons to see upon entering a bookstore. That is no longer the case. Internet retail stores such as Amazon use reviews as a ranking system. The more "good reviews", the higher a book climbs in rank. Unless a book title is created with search engines in mind by using key words, a new book will not be seen by potential buyers as it is buried beneath millions of other books titles.

Unfortunately, this system does not work well for most authors. The scales are unfairly tipped and not in the authors favor.

What happens is it is difficult to get good reviews without an established platform and fan base. Most readers that enjoy a book do not take the time to go leave a good review. However, there are hordes of readers that feel they are critics and enjoy leaving negative reviews, and this could be detrimental to book sales.

There are two types of people in the world, those that do and those that don't. George Bernard Shaw wrote, "Those who can do, and those who can't - teach."Critics are the same.

When an author writes, he or she exposes their soul to be judged by the world. It takes an enormous amount of courage to be a writer. Writers are like artists, what they produce comes from within and they are highly emotional and criticism is deeply heartfelt. Many talent writers have thrown away a career before it even began due to a bad review. Expect a bad review or two and do not to let them bother you. E.L James was crucified by reviewers for 50 Shades of Grey, but was able to laugh her way all the way to the bank.

How can an author tip the scale in his or her favor? It takes work and strategic ploys. All you need to do to quickly generate good reviews and climb the ranking system is be creative.

One way that has good results is to run a promotion with a free giveaway such as a new Kindle to verified purchasers that leave a positive review. Run it for 3 months and draw a name out of a hat to be fair. This can be done from a website or through a social media outlet such as Facebook, Twitter or Goodreads. You can include a temporary blurb on the Amazon sales page for your book or have it included at the opening of your book that requires the reader to submit their entry via email that includes his or her Amazon screen name to verify the positive review. A publisher (print on demand) can easily add and remove text from a book within a 24 hour period. People love the chance to get something for free and the cost of the prize is worth the long term benefits.

Independent Bookstores

The large bookstore chains may have toppled like dominoes, but the demand for printed books has brought forth a resurgence of indie bookstores. The "mom & pop" bookstores are flourishing, and this is good news to self published authors.

Most independent bookstores will be open to purchasing self published books. If not, they will most likely take the books on consignment.

Hasting's is a large retail chain that has survived the bookstore crash that leveled industry giants such as Borders. Hasting's will shelve self published books. The author signs a contract agreement for royalty payment and restocking books that are sold.

Empire Publishing

What sets Empire Publishing apart from the others? Empire is not only a publisher; the company is also a literary service bureau with the author's best interest as the foundation. By using Empire Publishing, the author is not bound to a contract nor is there any restrictions imposed on the author's work. What this means is the author maintains all rights, ownership and royalties. The author then has the freedom to continue publishing through other media's. This is beneficial to authors today and in the future as digital technology advances. It's as simple as the author owning the ISBN number for his or her work and not being obligated to a lengthy contract. Even better is the author gets the same service as a he or she would with a big name publisher.

You are in the driver's seat. Actually, we are so confident about our services, we encourage you to shop around before deciding how you want to go about making your publishing dream into a reality. We do not discriminate and believe everyone has a unique voice. With passion and a commitment to excellence, our agency brings heart and precision execution to each of our tailor-made marketing campaigns.

Empire Publishing offers more publishing packages than anyone that range from Free Publishing and Budget Publishing to multiple levels of High End Publishing. We have created a Publishing Package to meet any need and budget. Our packages are designed to help launch an author's career and not see their hard work never get off the ground.

Publishing Packages

Print and Digital Combo Bronze Package

Are you ready to get published and shopping for the easiest, most economical and best service available? Look no further. The "Bronze" combo-publishing package is designed for smaller books (less than 15,000 words) without skimping on quality. This is the ideal package for short stories. This package gives an author the freedom of choice to add-on services or upgrades at any time during and after the publishing process. Check the similar package offered by our competitors to see what you actually get for your money. They do not include an assigned bar code, eBook, personal eStore, distribution or an online account to monitor monthly sales for the same price as Empire Publishing's "Bronze" publishing package. You have the option of ordering as many books, at any time, for your personal use or for resale as you want at the low cost author discount or don't order any at all. From the beginning, Empire Publishing's goal has been to provide a way for any aspiring author to become published regardless of how little or how much they have to invest in themselves. Empire Publishing utilizes the popular Print on Demand and Distribution service. This means there is no inventory, buy backs nor money out of the author's pocket. Books are printed as ordered. Scroll down to Product Details and click on the "info" button for more information on what is included in each combo publishing package.

Print and Digital Combo Copper Package

The "Copper" combo-publishing package is entry level publishing package for books over 80,000 words without skimping on quality. This package gives an author the freedom of choice to add-on services or upgrades at any time during and after the publishing process.

Print and Digital Combo Silver Package

The "Silver" combo-publishing package includes upgrades on services, more custom cover options, interior options, trim sizes, larger page count, expanded distribution and promotional tools. This package is designed as to be an excellent starting point for authors without a substantial investment. Scroll down to Product Details and click on the "info" button for more information on what is included in each combo publishing package. Options are available to upgrade any service by adding on as a-la-cart items.

Print and Digital Combo Gold Package

The "Gold" combo-publishing package includes upgrades on services, more custom cover options, interior options, trim sizes, expanded distribution and promotional tools.

This package is designed for authors serious about launching a career in writing without spending a lot of money. The "Gold" combo-publishing package includes a personal assistant to assist in a marketing strategy. Also, included is social media development to begin building an author platform. As with all Empire Publishing packages, authors receive more for the money than what the other publishers are offering. Scroll down to Product Details and click on the "info" button for more information on what is included in each combo publishing package. Options are available to upgrade any service by adding on as a-la-cart items.

Print and Digital Combo Platinum Package
The "Platinum" combo-publishing package is the upper echelon of independent publishing. Includes upgrades on services, more custom cover options, interior options, trim sizes, expanded distribution and promotional tools. This package is designed for authors serious about launching a career in writing. The "Platinum" combo-publishing package includes everything needed to produce a professionally manufactured product (your book), establish an author platform and to market it in a fashion that will produce higher royalties.

Print and Digital Combo Titanium Package
The "Titanium" combo-publishing package is the ultimate in independent publishing package available.... anywhere. It includes the best of Empire Publishing services, custom cover, custom interior, expanded distribution and marketing tools. This package is designed for authors serious about launching a career in writing. The "Platinum" combo-publishing package includes everything needed to

produce a professionally manufactured product (your book), establish a solid author platform and market it in a fashion that will produce high royalties.

Premium eBook Publishing

Empire Publishing has designed the Premium Package for entry level and intermediate authors whom are serious about starting his or her career in the literary world. As authors ourselves, we at Empire Publishing want nothing more than to see you get there as easily and painlessly as possible. This package is one of the best for the money. We combined several professional services and then dropped the price to save you money and put you on your way to success. Our goal is to provide authors with the very best services for less, and you will never see us add useless fluff to make a package look more than it actually is as many other online publishers do to capitalize on those that don't know any better.

Platinum eBook Publishing

Empire Publishing has designed the Platinum Package for intermediate and pro authors whom are serious about advancing his or her writing skill into a lucrative career. It begins by taking that first huge step. As authors ourselves, we at Empire Publishing want nothing more than to see you get there as easily and painlessly as possible. This package is one of the best for the money. We've combined several professional services and then dropped the price to save you money and put you on your way to success.

Amazon Kindle "Budget" Publishing

Amazon's hand held reading device the "Kindle" revolutionized the publishing industry. Sadly, it led to the demise of large bookstore chains such as Borders. However, the Kindle has become a money making machine for authors and has opened up doors for writers that were sealed shut at one time. There are many authors that are capitalizing on the Kindle format by publishing small books under 20,000 words, and selling them for a couple dollars each and raking in good money. Either way, large novel or small book, publishing on Kindle is a must for any author. Empire Publishing has created several packages in order to meet the needs of all authors. The "budget" package is to get you published at a minimal cost. Your manuscript receives one round of mechanical formatting to meet Kindle requirements. You have a choice between a free basic cover or supplying your own complete cover design. If you do not have a cover and want more than a basic cover, we will even give you $50 off any of our cover design services after purchasing this package. We convert your files to the proper formats, create your Kindle account, upload all files, run a test to preview your ebook, and then guide you through setting up your royalty information.

Nook "Budget" Publishing

The "Nook" from Barnes & Noble is the second leading digital reader on the market and one author's should not overlook. Authors need to make their books available on as many devices as possible to gain maximum sales potential. Not doing so will limit your potential audience and drastically hamper book sales. Only books that have been submitted via the required process and format are available for Nook readers to purchase and enjoy. The Nook has a fantastic free reading app to download that allows readers to sync their account to other devices such as smartphones, tablets and computers. A reader can change devices and pick up where they last read. Get your book in the hands of millions of potential readers worldwide.

Free eBook Publishing

Empire Publishing wants to give every author the opportunity to get published. We know that there are many people, especially in this economy that just do not have the financial resources to publish a book on their own. It is very costly and now that traditional publishers are pulling back on signing new authors, it's almost impossible to get a contract. Even you were lucky enough to be offered one, it may not be the best route to go if you are looking to make money. Independent authors are raking in hundreds to thousands of dollars per month on Kindle ebooks alone. Don't be left out of this booming market. We are offering a start up publishing service to you with no out of pocket expense. Your eBook will also be available for PC download, Barnes & Nobel's Nook and on Apple readers such as the iPad and iPhone.

Print Only Publishing

On rare occasions, an author may only want a book in printed format. We have designed this package with those people in mind. At this time, only available in trade paperback. You can upgrade to a Premium Custom Cover add-on if you prefer custom designed cover and you will receive a 15% discount on that upgrade.

Traditional Publishing

If you have an exceptional story that is well polished, you might be eligible to receive a traditional publishing contract. That means no money out of your pocket and

Empire Publishing picks up the bill. Included is every service Empire Publishing has to offer which is far more than any traditional publisher provides to an author. Send query letter and synopsis to editor@empire-publishing.com

Free Publishing Contest
Empire Publishing wants to help get books out into the public that may never see the light of day otherwise. Every two months, we offer a Free Publishing package to a deserving author. to keep us from being inundated with manuscripts, we choose a topic or genre which will be different each time. All you have to do is send us your synopsis and the first four chapters to enter the contest. One winner will be chosen and that author will receive a publishing package that includes both print and Kindle versions of his or her book. Manuscript must me under 60,000 words. We will format the interior and design the cover. Empire Publishing takes no percentage of sales, zip, nada... nothing at all. The author keeps all his or her royalties. How cool is that?

For more information on what is included in each package visit www.empire-publishing.com

Exclusive Payment Program

Empire Publishing offers an exclusive payment plan to make it easier for authors to get published. Wherever you see the Payment Plan logo, that service can be provided by choosing either weekly or monthly repayments. Our goal is to help authors become published and we look for every possible way to make it easier for you.

Using the Payment Plan Service is simple. Just choose your service, choose either weekly or monthly repayments and we'll calculate your repayments with no hidden costs or interest. We offer 3 - 6 month payment plans depending on the service or publishing package.

Everyone Has a Voice. Empire Publishing is here to get Yours Heard.

What are you waiting for? Look around our website, shop around with others to see what they offer, and then let us turn your dream of being a published author into reality. We make it easy, quick, and hassle free. We stand beside our authors and will be there to assist you long after your work is published. We are constantly experimenting with unconventional methods of marketing, and as an Empire Publishing author, only you will be privy to that information. When you are ready, contact us, and we will get the ball rolling in the right direction for you.

www.empire-publishing.com

Empire ®
PUBLISHING

$20
REBATE

You will receive an instant $20 off when purchasing one of the selected Publishing Packages at Empire Publishing. Mail this voucher* to the address below and the savings will be applied upon purchase.**

Name _____

Address _____

Email _____

Send to:
Empire Publishing
13567 Fellows Avenue
Sylmar, California 91342

* Cut this page out of the booklet. Copies will not be accepted.
** This voucher is good for the Silver, Gold, Platinum and Titanium publishing packages.